I0797691

EARTH'S ENERGY RESOURCES

# WIND ENERGY

REBECCA FELIX

Consulting Editor, Diane Craig, M.A./Reading Specialist

Sandcastle

An Imprint of Abdo Publishing
abdopublishing.com

abdopublishing.com

Published by Abdo Publishing, a division of ABDO, PO Box 398166, Minneapolis, Minnesota 55439. 

Printed in the United States of America, North Mankato, Minnesota

052018
092018

THIS BOOK CONTAINS
RECYCLED MATERIALS

Design and Production: Mighty Media, Inc.
Editor: Liz Salzmann
Cover Photographs: Shutterstock
Interior Photographs: iStockphoto; Shutterstock; The Western Reserve Historical Society, Cleveland, Ohio; Wikimedia Commons

Library of Congress Control Number: 2017961705

**Publisher's Cataloging-in-Publication Data**
Name: Felix, Rebecca, author.
Title: Wind energy / by Rebecca Felix.
Description: Minneapolis, Minnesota : Abdo Publishing, 2019. | Series: Earth's energy resources
Identifiers: ISBN 9781532115585 (lib.bdg.) | ISBN 9781532156304 (ebook)
Subjects: LCSH: Wind power--Juvenile literature. | Power resources--Juvenile literature. | Wind energy conversion systems--Juvenile literature. | Energy harvesting--Juvenile literature. | Energy development--Juvenile literature.
Classification: DDC 333.92--dc23

**SandCastle™ Level: Fluent**

SandCastle™ books are created by a team of professional educators, reading specialists, and content developers around five essential components—phonemic awareness, phonics, vocabulary, text comprehension, and fluency—to assist young readers as they develop reading skills and strategies and increase their general knowledge. All books are written, reviewed, and leveled for guided reading, early reading intervention, and Accelerated Reader™ programs for use in shared, guided, and independent reading and writing activities to support a balanced approach to literacy instruction. The SandCastle™ series has four levels that correspond to early literacy development. The levels are provided to help teachers and parents select appropriate books for young readers.

**EMERGING · BEGINNING · TRANSITIONAL · FLUENT**

# CONTENTS

## ALL ABOUT WIND ENERGY

We use energy each day! It comes from many **sources**.

One **source** is the wind. It has **kinetic energy**.

Wind is a natural **resource**. Nature provides it. It is **renewable**.

People first built windmills long ago. Some have four blades.

Others have many blades.

The wind pushes the blades.
This turns the mill.

Windmills **grind** grain.
They **pump** water.

In 1888 Charles F. Brush used wind energy. Brush built a wind **turbine**.

It powered his house!

Most wind **turbines** today have three blades.

**Turbines** create electricity.
This is wind power.

A group of **turbines** is called a wind farm.

Wind farms produce a lot of electricity.

Wires bring the electricity to homes and businesses.

This electricity powers lights.
It powers **electronics**.

People are using wind energy more and more.

Many new **turbines** are built each year.

## THINK ABOUT IT

**In what new ways can we use wind energy?**

# GLOSSARY

**electronics** – products that operate using many small electrical parts.

**grind** – to crush something into a powder.

**kinetic energy** – energy that comes from motion.

**pump** – to move a liquid or a gas through a tube or a pipe.

**renewable** – able to be replaced by nature.

**resource** – something that is usable or valuable.

**source** – where something comes from or begins.

**turbine** – a machine that produces power when it is rotated at high speed.